HELEN PLUM MEMORIAL LIBRARY

3 1502 00758 0994

W9-ART-473

Pr

RIVERS
OF THE WORLD

THE
TIGRIS
AND
EUPHRATES
RIVERS

Earle Rice Jr.

HELEN PLUM
LIBRARY
LOMBARD, IL

Mitchell Lane
PUBLISHERS
P.O. Box 196
Hockessin, Delaware 19707

Y
915.67
RIC

RIVERS

OF THE WORLD

The Amazon River

The Nile River

The Ganges River

The Mississippi River

The Rhine River

The Tigris and Euphrates Rivers

The Yangtze River

The Volga River

Copyright © 2013 by Mitchell Lane Publishers

All rights reserved. No part of this book may be reproduced without written permission from the publisher. Printed and bound in the United States of America.

PUBLISHER'S NOTE: The facts on which the story in this book is based have been thoroughly researched. Documentation of such research can be found on page 44. While every possible effort has been made to ensure accuracy, the publisher will not assume liability for damages caused by inaccuracies in the data, and makes no warranty on the accuracy of the information contained herein.

Printing   1   2   3   4   5   6   7   8   9

Library of Congress
Cataloging-in-Publication Data
Rice, Earl.
  The Tigris and Euphrates rivers / by Earl Rice Jr.
      p. cm.—(Rivers of the world)
  Includes bibliographical references and index.
  ISBN 978-1-61228-298-5 (library bound)
  1. Tigris River—Juvenile literature. 2. Euphrates
River—Juvenile literature. I. Title.
  DS49.7.R54 2012
  956.7—dc23
                                                    2012009468

eBook ISBN: 9781612283715

PLB

3 1502 00758 0994

CONTENTS

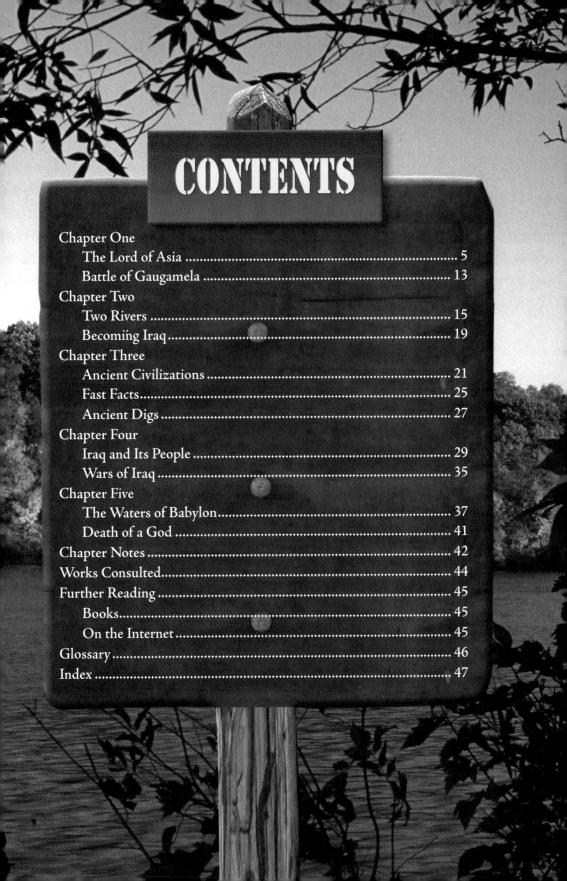

The Tigris River would await a showdown between Alexander the Great and the forces of the Persian king Darius III.

CHAPTER 1

The Lord of Asia

In early March 333 BCE, Alexander the Great arrived in Gordium. The town was the capital of ancient Phrygia in west-central Asia Minor (modern-day Turkey). Alexander was the greatest military leader of antiquity. His father was Philip II of Macedonia, who had dreamed of conquering all of the Persian Empire. Alexander had succeeded his father upon Philip's assassination in 336 BCE. He then led his army of Macedonians and Greeks in a campaign of conquest.

On the way to Gordium, Alexander defeated a hastily assembled Persian army at the Granicus River in Asia Minor in May 334 BCE. Alexander's victory represented the first step in fulfilling Philip's dream. Alexander immediately began a long march east and south through Asia Minor. Ten months later, he reached Gordium. The town was located about 50 miles (80 kilometers) west-southwest of modern Ankara, the capital of Turkey.

King Midas and his daughter

The kingdom of Phrygia was founded in the eighth century BCE by the peasant-king Gordius. It was later consolidated by his son Midas, the king famous for his golden touch. Gordius's burial site was marked by a ceremonial wagon that Midas had dedicated to the supreme Greek god Zeus. Four centuries later, it still stood on the acropolis (fortress) overlooking Gordium. According to legend, the wagon's yoke was tied to a beam with a rope of bark and a complex multiple knot which had no visible ends. An ancient seer had predicted that anyone who was able to undo the knot would become lord of all Asia.

Many men before Alexander had tried and failed to loosen the Gordian knot. Even so, Alexander could not resist the challenge. A large crowd gathered to witness his attempt to untie the knot. For a long time, Alexander struggled unsuccessfully to loosen the intricate knot. Failure, he knew, would hurt his reputation and lower the morale of his men. At last, in desperation, he shouted, "What difference does it make how I loose it?"[1] He drew his sword and slashed through the knot in a single stroke.

That night, lightning lit the sky and thunder boomed across the land. Alexander took the heavenly coincidence to mean Zeus's approval of his action. He felt that it boded well for his continuing campaign against the Persians. It also reinforced his belief that the gods watched over him. Whether the tale of Alexander and the Gordian knot is truth or fable is open to argument. But there can be no doubt that he was on his way to becoming the lord of Asia.

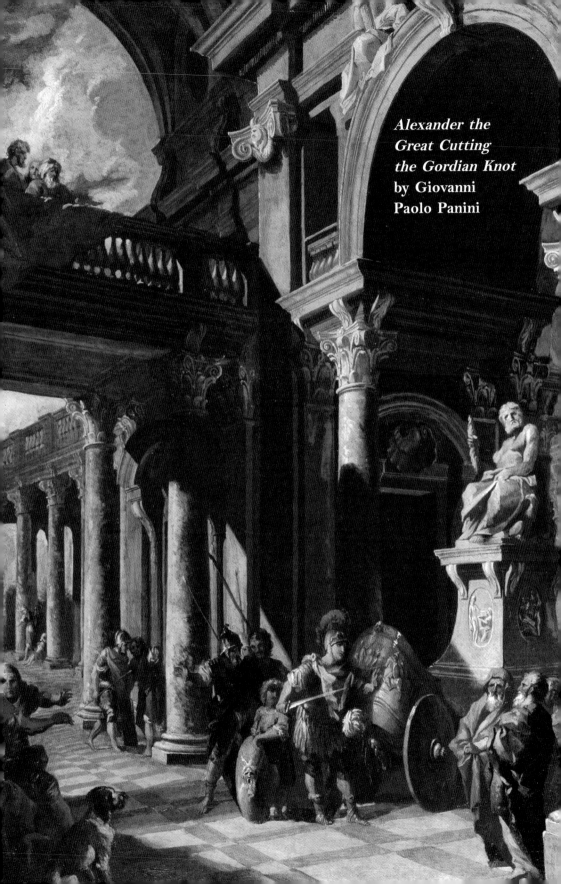

Alexander the Great Cutting the Gordian Knot by Giovanni Paolo Panini

Alexander left Gordium and led his army of 37,000 men across the mountainous wilderness of Cappadocia in east Asia Minor. He emerged from the Taurus Mountains and crossed the Cilician plain along the Mediterranean coastline. At Issus, near the Pinarus River, he found a Persian army of more than 100,000 men awaiting his arrival in November 333 BCE. It was led personally by Darius III, the king of Persia.

Before engaging the Persians, Alexander addressed his warriors to give them confidence. "Remember," he said, "that already danger has often threatened you and you have looked it triumphantly in the face; this time the struggle will be between a victorious army and an enemy

Early Roman mosaic of Alexander and the Persian king, Darius III, in the battle of Issus. Alexander is on the far left, Darius is in the chariot toward the center.

already once vanquished."[2] Through superior generalship, Alexander outmaneuvered and defeated the larger Persian force. Darius fled to avoid capture.

Alexander did not immediately pursue his fleeing enemy. Instead, he spent most of the next two years expanding his growing empire. He followed the Mediterranean coastline far into Egypt. Early in 332 BCE, he founded the city of Alexandria. Late that year, he began his reign as pharaoh, or ruler, of Egypt.

Word reached Alexander in April of 331 BCE that Darius had assembled an army for a decisive battle on the Plain of Gaugamela in

Mesopotamia (modern-day Iraq). Mesopotamia—which comes from the Greek and means "between the rivers"—was an ancient land as old as time. "Bracketed by the Euphrates River on the west and the Tigris on the east, it had always been a fabled place," writes historian Laura Foreman, "figuring in the rise and fall of empires, and for more than two centuries it had been the epicenter of Persian wealth and power."[3]

Alexander turned eastward to meet the Persian "king of all lands" with an army now numbering about 47,000 men. Over the next six months, Alexander led his army overland across Syria and into Mesopotamia. He crossed both the Euphrates and Tigris rivers. With the coming of Alexander's army in late September 331 BCE, the storied old land was about to play host to yet another fallen empire. Darius may have felt the presence of an irresistible force. He sent a peace proposal to Alexander, who was then camped about seven miles north of Gaugamela. The Persian king offered Alexander all the land west of the Euphrates, his daughter as a bride to Alexander, royal marriage, and a large sum of ransom money as a peace settlement.

Alexander the Great

This large Flemish tapestry, from the first half of the 18th century, shows the warriors at the Battle of Gaugamela.

Parmenio, one of Alexander's generals, thought Darius's offer was most generous. "If I were Alexander," he said, "I should accept this offer."[4]

"So should I," Alexander replied, "if I were Parmenio."[5] He sent word to Darius: Asia was not big enough for the two of them. If Darius wanted to keep his throne, he would have to fight for it. The Battle of Gaugamela commenced on October 1, 331 BCE.

In Persepolis, the capital of the Persian Empire, Alexander's troops target the main palace for looting and pillaging. Upon his victory over the Persians, he burned and destroyed many structures and stole their treasures.

The battle ended in Alexander's third, and most decisive, victory over the Persians. His triumph opened Mesopotamia to the lasting influence of the Western World. "The new world heralded by Alexander," observed historian Georges Roux, "was a fast changing world bent on extensive commercial intercourse, bursting with curiosity, eager to reappraise most of its religious, moral, scientific, and artistic values."[6]

Battle of Gaugamela

Darius III

After losing the Battle of Issus in November 333 BCE, Darius III had almost two years to get ready for his final clash with Alexander the Great. He used the time to build an army that may have been as large as 245,000 men—200,000 infantry and 45,000 cavalry. Darius relied heavily on 200 chariots fitted with scythes and 15 war elephants to return a victory in the battle to come.

Darius selected a setting where his greater numbers would work to his best advantage. He positioned his army on the left bank of the Tigris River on a large open plain near the village of Gaugamela. Alexander arrived at the high ground overlooking the plain at the end of September 331 BCE. His army of 40,000 infantry and 7,000 cavalry put him at a significant disadvantage. Parmenio suggested a night attack to counter the odds. Alexander said, "I will not demean myself by stealing victory like a thief."[7]

On the morning of October 1, Alexander entered the plain. He deployed his troops with his infantry centered in a phalanx (ranks and files) and his cavalry on the wings. Advancing obliquely to his right, he skirted the terrain leveled for the Persian scythe-chariots. Darius tried and failed to outflank him on the right. Alexander then struck hard and fast and broke the Persian center.

Darius again fled the battlefield. He was later killed by a group of his own troops. Alexander subsequently extended his empire eastward almost to the river Ganges in modern-day India.

The Tigris River at Diyarbakir in modern-day Turkey marks the beginning of the "Fertile Crescent."

CHAPTER 2

Two Rivers

Mesopotamia is the region between the Tigris and Euphrates rivers. It extends from the mountains of Asia Minor in the north to the Persian Gulf in the south. The plain between and around the Tigris and Euphrates rivers forms a semicircle of land called the "Fertile Crescent." The Crescent starts at the southeastern shore of the Mediterranean and arcs across the Syrian Desert and Iraq to the Persian Gulf.

From ancient Mesopotamia to modern Iraq, the land has owed most of its fertility to the nourishing waters of the Tigris-Euphrates river system. As aptly stated by professors Benjamin R. Foster and Karen Polinger Foster, "Ancient Iraq is the gift of two rivers."[1] Much the same might be said about modern Iraq.

People often think of the Tigris and the Euphrates as a single river. Both rivers originate within 50 miles (80 kilometers) of each other on the Anatolian plateau in eastern Turkey. It is basically a large plateau with mountains separating it from southeastern Europe and western Asia. In ancient

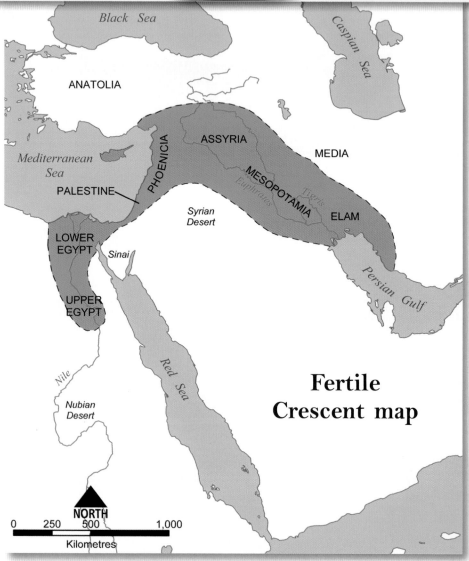

Fertile Crescent map

times, Anatolia's vast network of trade routes served as well-traveled crossroads for caravans linking the East and the West.

The Tigris rises out of Lake Hazar in the Taurus Mountains. It flows southeasterly for 1,180 miles (1,899 km). Along its course, it passes Diyarbakir in Turkey, and Mosul and Baghdad in Iraq. Several tributaries join it on its left bank. Of these, the most notable are the Great Zab, Little Zab, and Diyala in Iraq.

Diyarbakir derives its name from the copper ore existing in the area. Black basalt walls surrounding the city lend it a medieval air. Next to China's Great Wall, they are the largest and best preserved ancient walls in the world. They are 39 feet (12 meters) high and between 10 to 16 feet (3 to 5 meters) wide. The walls date back to early Byzantine times. They contain five gates, sixteen keeps (or strong points), and 82 watchtowers. Diyarbakir lies in a transition zone connecting the mountainous northern region with the plains of Mesopotamia.

Beyond Diyarbakir, the Tigris forms a 20-mile (32-kilometer) stretch of the border between Turkey and Syria. Continuing its southeasterly flow down through the barren countryside of northern Iraq, the Tigris next arrives at the city of Mosul. Once an important stop for trade caravans out of Iran, Mosul remains a chief Iraqi trading center. Local oil refineries process oil produced nearby. Various mosques, churches, shrines, and historical buildings help to illuminate the city's past.

Across the river from Mosul, the ruins of ancient Nineveh recall the realities of a long-dead empire. Once called "the bloody city of lies and robbery,"[2] the former capital of the empire of Assyria was rebuilt and given new life by King Sennacherib in the seventh century BCE. Excavations begun by Sir Austen Henry Layard in 1845 revealed palaces, a library, and city walls with numerous gates.

Next in view along the river's course stands the medieval city of Samarra. Its name in Arabic means "a joy for all who see." Known for its towering minaret, it served as the residence of Abbasids, the rulers of the Muslim Empire in the ninth century. Shiite Muslims consider the city sacred. Samarra contains the mausoleums of the tenth and eleventh imams, who were spiritual leaders of the Twelver sect of Shiite Muslims. It also contains a shrine to Muhammad al-Mahdi. He was the twelfth and final imam of the Twelvers.

Seventy-eight miles (126 kilometers) farther south, the Tigris flows through the center of Baghdad, the capital of Iraq. This frequently troubled city was almost completely destroyed by the Mongols in 1258. Timur, the Turkic ruler, conquered it in 1401. Suleyman the Magnificent captured it in 1534. And British troops seized it in 1917. The Iraqi monarchy was overthrown by an army coup in Baghdad in 1958. More recently, the city was severely damaged by bombing during the Gulf War in 1991 and the Iraq War in 2003. In spite of its calamities, Baghdad continues to persevere.

South of Baghdad, the Tigris veers to the east and enters the immense alluvial lowlands of southern Mesopotamia. The region consists of about 10,000 square miles (25,600 square kilometers) formed by soil and sand deposits from the Tigris-Euphrates river system.

To the west of the Tigris, the Euphrates is formed by the confluence of two rivers—the Murat Nehri (or Eastern Euphrates) and the Karasu (or Western Euphrates) in Turkey. It flows south and southeasterly for 2,235 miles (3,596 kilometers). Its course crosses Turkey and northeast Syria through rocky gorges and passes through the deserts of west and central Iraq. Other than the Balikh and Khabur rivers beyond the Syrian town of Dayr az Zawr (DARE-eez ZOR), the Euphrates receives hardly any important tributaries.

Flowing through a wide valley irrigated by waterwheels, the Euphrates moves on toward the Iraqi town of Hit, about 90 miles (145 kilometers) west of Baghdad. This old town is located on the west side of a triangular limestone plateau known as Al-Jazirah (Arabic for "the island").

After Hit, the Euphrates bends eastward and borders the alluvial plain it shares with the Tigris. Below the town of Al Musayyib, the river splits into two branches—Al Hindiyah and Al Hillah. These offshoots rejoin the river proper at the town of Samawa. Also at this point, the Baghdad-Basra railroad crosses the Euphrates.

At Al Qurnah, the Euphrates converges with the Tigris to form the Shatt al Arab (Arabic River or "stream of the Arabs"). Many scholars believe Al Qurnah is the site of the Biblical Garden of Eden where human life began. Forty-five miles (72 kilometers) downriver, the Shatt al Arab flows through Basra—Iraq's only seaport—and empties into the Persian Gulf.

Becoming Iraq

King Faisal I

Today's Iraq occupies 168,927 square miles (437,521 square kilometers) of the land known for ages as Mesopotamia. The Ottoman Empire (present-day Turkey) seized control over Mesopotamia in the early 1500s. During World War I, the British campaigned against the Ottoman Turks in both Palestine and Mesopotamia. By the end of the war in 1918, the British controlled most of the region.

In 1920, the League of Nations issued a mandate for Mesopotamia to be ruled under British administration. The following year, Britain renamed the country Iraq and established Faisal I as its king. British control ended in 1932 as Iraq became an independent nation. Faisal II took full power at the age of eighteen in 1953.

Opposition to the monarchy by Pan-Arabism activists grew steadily over the next five years. In 1958, army officers overthrew Faisal. They established the Republic of Iraq. Faisal was executed and General Abdul Karim Qasim was named Iraq's premier.

Qasim fell victim to the same fate when Army officers executed him in 1963. Pan-Arabism activists led by members of the Ba'ath Party installed Abdul Salam Arif as president. He died in an airplane crash three years later and his brother, Abdul Rahman Arif, succeeded him. He was overthrown by Baathist Ahmad Hasan al-Bakr in 1968. Bakr served until 1979, when he resigned. A rising Ba'athist star named Saddam Hussein succeeded him. After a brutal 24-year reign, Saddam was removed from power during the Iraq War in 2003, tried, and finally executed in 2006. Iraq is now striving to become a free and democratic nation.

Ziggurat of Ur, Iraq

CHAPTER 3

Ancient Civilizations

Human life has existed by the Tigris and Euphrates rivers for about 10,000 years. The first people to arrive in the region were nomads. These were wanderers who lived by hunting, fishing, and gathering grains and wild plants. As their numbers grew, they began to settle. They built dwellings of sun-baked clay bricks.

Over time, small villages grew into large cities. These cities were usually built around a ziggurat. A ziggurat was a pyramidal temple tower with outside staircases. Each city had a local god served by priests. The temple had a shrine to the local god on top. Cities became city-states and eventually gave rise to great civilizations. Mesopotamia became known as the "cradle of civilization."

Early civilizations in Mesopotamia included the kingdoms of Sumer, Akkad, Babylonia, and Assyria. Sumer was the site of the earliest known civilization. It was located between the Tigris and Euphrates

rivers, from about present-day Baghdad to the Persian Gulf. This region later became Babylonia.

A non-Semitic people called Ubaidians first settled in Sumer around 5000 to 4500 BCE. (According to tradition, Semites are people descended from Shem, one of three sons of the Biblical Noah. They were mostly Jews, Arabs, Assyrians, and Phoenicians.) The people known as Sumerians first arrived in Sumer about 3300 BCE. They probably came from Anatolia.

Sumerians developed the first true cities about 3000 BCE. These cities evolved into at least 12 city-states. They were loosely unified

Sumerian ziggurats were built so high that they resembled the surrounding mountains of the region.

under the alternating rule of kings from a given city-state. Each city-state kept written records with the first known system of writing, which is called cuneiform. Sumerians used this system to inscribe wedge-shaped characters in clay tablets with a stylus. Notable among the city-states were Kish, Erech, Ur, Nippur, and Lagash. Ur was the most famous of them all. The Bible identifies Ur as the city of Abraham. He is considered to be the father of the Jewish people.

Sumerians engaged in such activities as metalworking, pottery, trade, hunting, fishing, and irrigated agriculture. They raised crops such as barley, flax, beans, wheat, grapes, and olives. And they successfully domesticated donkeys, goats, and sheep. Their innovations included the wheel, the plow, the sickle, and published codes of laws.

Sumer fought and gradually united with Akkad to its immediate north. Sargon of Akkad became the first to govern the city-states as a truly unified entity. He reigned from c. 2334 to 2279 BCE. His dynasty collapsed after about a hundred years. The city-states reverted to an independent status until reunited under Ur-Nammu (c. 2112–2095 BCE).

According to historian Georges Roux, Ur-Nammu was long "thought to have dictated what is considered to be the most ancient collection of laws in the world."[1] However, as Roux noted, "it appears from a newly found tablet that the true author was his son Shulgi."[2] These laws gave evidence of a polished and civilized society.

"Ur-Nammu also revived agriculture and improved communications," added Roux, "by digging a number of canals; towns were fortified against future wars, and an enormous amount of rebuilding was carried out."[3] During the final Ur dynasty, Sumer declined under internal pressures and external incursions.

While Sumer and Akkad fought and eventually merged, the Amorites swept in from Syria or Arabia. They were a western Semitic tribe. By 1900 BCE, they had conquered all of Mesopotamia. The Amorites established a new empire between the twin rivers called Babylonia. They ruled for the next three hundred years.

Ancient Babylon of Mesopotamia was located between the Tigris and Euphrates rivers. The ruins of the city can be found just south of Baghdad.

Babylon was Babylonia's greatest city. It was located on the Euphrates, about 56 miles (90 kilometers) south of present-day Baghdad. An outer wall surrounded the city. It measured 10 miles (16 kilometers) around, 50 feet (15 meters) high, and 55 feet (17 meters) thick. Huge bronze gates controlled passage in and out of the city. Babylon became the political, commercial, and religious heart of the Babylonian empire.

Hammurabi, who served as king from 1792 to 1750, was probably the most famous Babylonian ruler. "From his modest base in the city of

FAST FACTS

- The 2,235-mile-long (3,596 kilometers) Euphrates is the longest river in southwestern Asia.

- The Tigris is the second longest river in southwestern Asia at a length of 1,180 miles (1,899 kilometers).

- At Kut, the Tigris is about 1,300 feet (396 meters) wide, with a depth ranging from a normal 4.5 feet (1.37 meters) to 26 feet (8 meters) when flooding.

- At Amara, the Tigris is only 600 feet (183 meters) wide, with a depth varying from a normal 6.5 feet (2 meters) to 13 feet (4 meters) when flooding.

- The Shatt al Arab is 30 feet (9 meters) deep and more than 760 feet (232 meters) wide at Basra. The width increases to about half a mile (800 meters) at its mouth.

- Two types of boats are used on the Tigris and Shatt al Arab—a round skin boat called a coracle, and a rectangular type of raft known as a riverboat.

- Many scholars believe the Ma'dan, or Marsh Arabs, provide a link to the ancient Sumerians but the Ma'dan left no written records to affirm that belief.

- Nearly 70 percent of the karez system of underground aqueducts in northern Iraq has dried up in the past four years.

- Iraq was once a prominent wheat exporter, but a water crisis has turned the nation into one of the world's largest wheat importers.

- The original Sumerian name for the Tigris was Idigna, which can be interpreted as "the swift river."

- The Sumerian script had about 500 wedge-shaped characters.

Babylon," write professors Benjamin and Karen Foster, "he craftily built an empire using brute force, alliance, and betrayal."[4] More than once, he turned on former allies and defeated them. He justified his treachery by claiming the approval of the gods of the city-states he conquered. He boasted, "I brought happiness to the people, I made all the people of the realm lie down in green pastures, I allowed no one to alarm them."[5]

Under Hammurabi, Babylon prospered. Crops, flocks, and trade flourished. He promoted science and learning and encouraged religion. Babylonians worshipped their own gods and also those of the Sumerians and Akkadians. Of Hammurabi's many accomplishments, he is perhaps best remembered for his code of law. The Code of Hammurabi is inscribed on a block of black basalt. It consists of 282 laws covering a vast range of social conduct.

After Hammurabi's death in 1750 BCE, Babylonia declined and was finally destroyed by Assyrian King Sennacherib in 689 BCE. In 607 BCE, however, Chaldean ruler Nebuchadnezzar II rebuilt and revitalized the city. History credits him with building the Hanging Gardens of Babylon. It was one of the Seven Wonders of the Ancient World.

The Persians captured Babylonia in 539 BCE. Shortly after Alexander the Great defeated the Persian Empire in 331 BCE, his successors abandoned Babylon. Thereafter, one of the world's greatest empires slipped quietly into history.

Meanwhile, to the north, Assyria thrived in the second millennium BCE. It began as a dependency of Babylonia and later of the kingdom of Mitanni. Assyrians were known for their fighting prowess. Under several strong kings based in Nineveh, they united most of the Middle East. But they died as they had lived—by the sword.

Beginning in 612 BCE, a coalition of Chaldean and Mede invaders toppled Assyria's cities one by one. By 609 BCE, the Assyrian Empire ceased to exist. Assyrians left behind a warrior tradition and a legacy of monument building at once-thriving cities such as Nineveh, Ashur, and Nimrud.

Ancient Digs

Cuneiform tablet

People today owe much of their knowledge of the past to the writings and artifacts left behind by earlier civilizations. Ancient scribes recorded their histories in writing systems using pictures and symbols. Typical artifacts (things created by humans) include such items as tools, weapons, eating utensils, pottery, and so on. Ancient writings and artifacts are usually found by archaeologists at excavation sites called "digs." Excavations at the sites of ancient Nineveh and Ur revealed valuable information about the Sumerians and the Assyrians, respectively.

In 1849, a British archaeologist made a startling discovery at Nineveh. Previous attempts to decipher Babylonian cuneiform writings had failed. "The turning point came," according to professors Benjamin and Karen Foster, "after Austen Henry Layard unearthed at Nineveh thousands of cuneiform tablets from the library of Assurbanipal."[6] Later, four scholars conducted separate translations of the same tablets. Similar results validated their efforts. Babylonian could now be read.

Between 1922 and 1934, British archaeologist Sir Leonard Woolley uncovered a massive grave at Ur. It contained the king and queen of the First Dynasty. "He found the king buried with three retainers," wrote historian C. B. Falls, "and in an adjoining vault there were sixty-two more—a body-guard of death."[7] The queen's attendants added another twenty-five men and women. "There were no signs of violence or terror," added Falls. "It was a tableau of silence."[8] Woolley also discovered various artifacts showing the wealth and art of Sumer.

Tigris River at Diyarbakir

Iraq and Its People

Alexander the Great died in Babylon in 323 BCE. Greek rule in Mesopotamia ended soon afterward. The land was subsequently ruled by Parthians, Romans, Persians, Arab Muslims, Mongols, Ottoman Turks, and finally the British. Then Mesopotamia gained its independence and took the name of Iraq in 1932. In less than a century, it has suffered the torment and destruction of three major wars and the tyranny of oppressive governments. Its history of turbulence has continued to this day.

Iraq includes most of old Mesopotamia. It borders Turkey in the north, Iran in the east, Kuwait, Saudi Arabia and the Persian Gulf in the south, and Jordan and Syria in the west. It has four major land regions—the mountains, the northern plain, the desert, and the southern plain. The upper, middle, and lower courses of the Tigris and Euphrates rivers flow through the mountains, northern plain, and southern plain, respectively.

The mountains of northeast Iraq form part of a range called the Zagros in Iran and the Taurus in Turkey. Elevations range from 6,000 feet to 10,000 feet (1,800 to 3,000 meters). Kurds—a stateless ethnic group close to Iranians—live in this lofty region. "The scenery was wild and beautiful," wrote explorer Wilfred Thesiger in the mid-1900s, "and the Kurds who lived there still wore the finery of tribal dress."[1] Kurds were promised their independence when the Ottoman Empire was dissolved in 1920. However, self-rule continues to elude them.

The northern plain lies between the Tigris and Euphrates rivers north of the city of Samarra. It is a region of dry, rolling land. Elevations vary from 1,200 feet (370 meters) in the foothills to 170 feet (50 meters) above sea level in the southern plain. A few farming villages dot the landscape of the otherwise bleak countryside.

Iraq's desert covers its western and southwestern region. It forms an extension of the larger Syrian Desert that stretches into Syria, Jordan, and Saudi Arabia. This barren region consists mostly of limestone hills and sand dunes. Depressions known as *wadis* are scattered across the desert. They are dry most of the year but become rivers after a rain.

The southern plain begins south of the city of Samarra and extends to the Persian Gulf. This region includes the fertile delta of the twin rivers that supports a large Iraqi population. Dams and irrigation systems control the flow of water that enhances farming productivity. This has enabled the growth of permanent populations, especially near Al Kut, 100 miles (161 kilometers) southeast of Baghdad. Crops grown in Iraq include barley, rice, wheat, dates, grapes, and tomatoes.

Marshlands cover much of the region to the south and east of Al Kut. The region is home to the Ma'dan or Marsh Arabs. Ma'dan means "dweller in the plains." Some Marsh Arabs cultivate crops such as rice, barley, wheat, and pearl millet. Others raise water buffaloes, spear fish, and produce woven products.

Papyrus, lotus, and tall reeds carpet the waterways with a thick underbrush. And willow, poplar, and alder trees abound in the level landscape. Hunters find a wealth of wild ducks, geese, and partridge in

The rivers create the marshes of southern Iraq, where Marsh Arabs pole their mashoofs along the waters.

Falconing is still practiced in Iraq, with annual events like festivals to celebrate this traditional method of hunting.

the wetlands. Falcons are trained for hunting. Owls, vultures, and ravens live near the Euphrates. Other wildlife includes antelope, gazelles, foxes, jackals, hyenas, porcupines, moles, jerboas, desert hares, and bats. Beavers, wild asses, and ostriches are rare.

In 1964, Wilfred Thesiger predicted the eventual destruction of the marshlands: "Soon the Marshes will probably be drained; when this happens, a way of life that has lasted for thousands of years will disappear."[2] After the Gulf War (1991), Saddam Hussein ordered a huge canal built to drain up to 90 percent of the marshes. Today, more than 50 percent of the 1970 levels have been restored, but the existence of the marshes remains at risk.

Climate across the four land regions ranges from moderate in the north to semitropical in the south and southeast. High temperatures average more than 100° F (32° C) in the summer. Winter lows drop to about 35° F (2° C) in the desert and in the north. Average annual precipitation ranges from 5 inches (13 centimeters) of rain in the desert to 15 inches (38 centimeters) of rain and snow in northern mountains. Precipitation occurs mostly between November and April.

Iraq's fast-growing population stood in July 2012 at slightly over 31,000,000, according to estimates in the *CIA World Factbook*. Roughly three-quarters of its people live in the southern plain. Seventy-five percent of Iraqis are Arab. Kurds make up another 20 percent. Other ethnic groups include Armenians, Assyrians, Turkomans, and Yazidis (Indo-Iranians). About 95 percent of all Iraqis are Muslim. More than half of them—about 60 to 65 percent—are Shiites; the rest belong to the Sunni branch of Islam. Iraqis speak Arabic throughout Iraq. Kurds in the north speak Kurdish. Both Arabic and Kurdish are official languages in Iraq.

Petrochemical production and oil refining represent Iraq's major industry. Some of Iraq's largest oil fields are located between the Shatt al Arab and the Kuwaiti border in the south, and west of the city of

Iraq gets much attention throughout the world from many other countries due to its large amount of oil refineries.

A boy rests on the banks of a dried-out section of the Euphrates River.

Kirkuk in the north. Other natural resources mined in Iraq include natural gas, sulfur, and phosphates. The ravages of war interrupted Iraq's oil production, but oil exports have returned to prewar levels. Some 30 million date palms produce another of Iraq's most important exports. Of all of its natural resources, however, none is so important as water.

The survival of Iraq and its people depends on their access to the life-sustaining waters of the Tigris and Euphrates rivers. But those waters are being reduced to a trickle. And the Fertile Crescent is threatened with extinction.

Wars of Iraq

Saddam Hussein

Over the last three decades, Iraq and its people have fought, suffered, and sacrificed in three major wars: the Iran-Iraq War (1980–1988), the Persian Gulf War (1991), and the Iraq War (2003). All three wars are directly attributable to Iraq's late oppressive leader, President Saddam Hussein. They arose from his fierce ambition and overreaching aims.

Saddam dreamed of controlling all the Gulf Arab states. After the overthrow of the Shah of Iran in 1979, Ayatollah Ruhollah Khomeini threatened to export Iran's religious revolution to neighboring Islamic countries. Saddam acted quickly to dispose of the potential threat. He invaded Iran in September 1980. A long war—costly to both nations—followed. It ended with a United Nations–sponsored cease-fire in August, 1988.

Iraq's war-weakened economy led Saddam to try to solve his financial problems through further aggression. On August 2, 1990, he seized a disputed portion of a Kuwaiti oil field and annexed Kuwait as a "lost province." World opinion turned against Saddam. Commencing in August 1990, a U.S.-led coalition brought the Persian Gulf War to a swift conclusion when ground forces began operations the following January. Just over a month later, Saddam surrendered, though he remained in power.

The Iraq War erupted with a devastating air attack on Baghdad by U.S.-led coalition forces on March 20, 2003. United States officials stated that the military campaign was aimed at eliminating Iraq's weapons of mass destruction and its ability to produce them. The United States declared the end of military operations on May 1, 2003. American troops captured Saddam in December, 2003. He was later tried and hanged.

The farms of Iraq greatly depend on irrigation from the rivers.

CHAPTER 5

The Waters of Babylon

"The ancient Fertile Crescent will disappear in this century," forecasts Akio Kitoh of Japan's Meteorological Research Institute. "The process has already begun."[1] Severe drought over the past several years has helped to accelerate the crisis. Some experts blame drought conditions on climate change. One study of the Fertile Crescent's future under climate change suggests flow on the Euphrates could fall by 73 percent.

Traditionally, Iraq has had more water than most other countries of the Middle East. Advanced early civilizations rose by the waters of Babylon. They developed the organization and technology needed to harness those waters. Archaeologists estimate that the development of irrigation systems reached a high point about 500 CE.

A network of irrigation and drainage canals made widespread cultivation possible. The land between the rivers turned into a food basket. But poor maintenance allowed the canal network to deteriorate by the 12th century. The Mongols destroyed what was left of it in the 13th century. It remained in a state of disrepair for hundreds of years. Iraq finally began an effort to restore the network in the 20th century. Part of the effort was aimed at controlling seasonal flooding.

Iraq constructed several large dams and barrages, repaired old canals, and built new irrigation systems. Dams also harnessed the energy from the force of water flow to produce hydroelectricity. (A dam stores water in a reservoir; a barrage diverts the flow of water but does not store it. Other structures that divert or control water flow are weirs and regulators. They are sometimes referred to as "dams.") Baghdad—which is only 112 feet (34 meters) above sea level—highlighted the need to control water flow.

"The Tharthar reservoir was planned in the 1950s to protect Baghdad from the ravages of the periodic flooding of the Tigris by storing extra water discharge upstream of the Samarra barrage," according to an article prepared by Providence College. "A derivation canal that links the Tigris to the Euphrates through the Tharthar Valley has been realized and operative since 1988."[2] Currently, there are 12 dams in the Tigris basin and six in the Euphrates basin. Six dams are operating in the waterways connecting the two rivers. "Thus both rivers are connected with each other far before [Shatt al Arab]."[3]

Iraq's farmland makes up one-fifth of its territory. About half of all its cultivated area is located in the northeastern plains and mountain valleys. The rest is in the valleys of the Tigris and Euphrates rivers. Enough rain falls at the higher elevations to sustain agriculture. Lower elevations receive scant rainfall. They rely instead on water from the rivers. Both rivers feed off the snowpack and rainfall in eastern Turkey and northwest Iran. River flow varies from year to year. High flow contributes to flooding. Conversely, low flow increases irrigation and farming difficulties.

Geographic factors add to Iraq's water problems. All rivers carry silt, which is sediment composed of small particles of sand and rock, downstream. The Tigris and Euphrates rivers deposit large amounts of silt in river channels, in canals, and on the flood plains. Silt has a high saline content. Added to an already salty soil, silt increases the need for good drainage. Iraq's flat plains make irrigation easier. But their susceptibility to flooding hampers drainage. Saltwater intrusion caused by drought and reduced water flow adds to Iraq's water problems.

Syria and Turkey both completed large dams on the Euphrates and filled large reservoirs upstream from Iraq in the early 1970s. The dams store enough water to ensure a constant supply of water. Iraqi officials protested the resultant lessening of water flow. They claimed irrigated areas along the Euphrates dropped from 336,056 acres (136,000 hectares) to 24,710 acres (10,000 hectares) from 1974 to 1975. Existing cordial relations between Turkey and Iraq continued with Turkey's assurance that things would get better.

Syria completed the Tabaqah Dam on the Euphrates in 1973. Purportedly, the dam produced 30 percent of the country's electricity.

The dam on the Euphrates has led to Syria and Turkey having a 30-year quarrel over the water of the Euphrates River and is among one of the Middle East's longest ongoing disputes.

Iraq was again adversely impacted. The reduced water flow kept some three million Iraqi farmers from irrigating their fields. And Iraq's water problems continued to worsen.

Cordial relations between Turkey and Iraq began to wear thin in the 1980s when Turkey began the Southeastern Anatolia Project. Commonly known as GAP (an acronym formed from its name in Turkish), its master plan calls for the construction of 22 dams, 19 power plants, and seven airports. Perhaps the most impressive of the dams is the Ataturk Dam, completed in 1990. It stands 554.5 feet (169 meters) high and extends over a length of 5,971 feet (1,820 meters). Its hydroelectric power plant has an installed power capacity of 2,400 megawatts.

GAP's basic aim is to raise incomes and living standards in the region, while providing social stability and enhancing growth. Turkish visionaries hope to achieve these goals through the jobs and production generated in the rural sector by this massive project. Turkey had planned to complete GAP by 2005, but work fell behind schedule. Construction on the project presently remains ongoing.

Both Syria and Iraq fear that GAP's ultimate effects will reduce their share of river water to unacceptable levels. Possible climate change and severe drought in 2008 and 2009 have abetted the deepening water crisis. A report by the United Nations Education, Scientific, and Cultural Organization (UNESCO) indicates "that more than 100,000 people in northern Iraq have fled their homes since 2005 because of inadequate water supplies."[4]

Time is running out on the Fertile Crescent. Hope remains high that Turkey and its neighbors can agree on fair water rights to the Tigris and Euphrates. Otherwise, the potential for water wars might become a reality. And the waters of Babylon could recede into history.

Death of a God

Alexander

After defeating the Persians at Gaugamela, Alexander the Great marched his army south. He crossed the Tigris again and entered Babylon on the Euphrates. A great victory celebration ensued in the ancient city. "Gleaming, broad-walled Babylon was renowned for its good wine, fine food, and gorgeous and obliging women," writes author Laura Foreman. "All these the Macedonians enjoyed—and all were freely given."[5] But Alexander's warriors had little time to rejoice. Their leader's thirst for conquest remained unslaked.

Alexander pressed on eastward. He crossed the Hindu Kush mountain range and advanced deep into India. He wanted to reach the river Ganges, which he considered to be the end of the known world. His battle-weary army rebelled, however, and threatened to mutiny. They had been away from home for almost a decade. Coenus, one of Alexander's old generals, finally said to him, "Sir, if there is one thing above all others a successful man should know, it is when to stop."[6] Alexander returned to Babylon.

In 324 BCE, Alexander sent word to the Greek states that he now and evermore wished to be publicly recognized as the son of Zeus, the "father of Gods and men." Even the stubborn Spartans agreed, declaring, "Let Alexander be a god if he wants to."[7]

Back in Babylon, Alexander began drinking to excess. After a drinking match one night, he fell ill. Eleven days later, the greatest conqueror the world has ever known died beside the rivers of Babylon. The veil of time shrouds the cause of his death, but the self-proclaimed god lives on in the annals of human conquest.

Chapter 1   The Lord of Asia

1. Laura Foreman, *Alexander the Conqueror: The Epic Story of the Warrior King* (Cambridge, Massachusetts: Da Capo Press, 2004), p. 92.
2. Arrian, *The Campaigns of Alexander.* Revised Edition. Translated by Aubrey de Sélincourt (New York: Penguin Books, 1971), p. 112.
3. Foreman, p. 134.
4. Peter Green, *Alexander of Macedon, 356–323 B.C.: A Historical Biography* (Berkeley, California: University of California Press, 1991), p. 287.
5. Ibid.
6. Georges Roux, *Ancient Iraq.* Third Edition (New York: Penguin Books, 1992), p. 424.
7. Arrian, p. 163.

Chapter 2   Two Rivers

1. Benjamin R. Foster and Karen Polinger Foster, *Civilizations of Ancient Iraq* (Princeton, New Jersey: Princeton University Press, 2009), p. 1.
2. C. B. Falls, *The First 3000 Years: Ancient Civilization of the Tigris, Euphrates, and Nile River Valleys, and the Mediterranean Sea* (New York: Viking Press, 1960), p. 130.

Chapter 3   Ancient Civilizations

1. Georges Roux, *Ancient Iraq.* Third Edition (New York: Penguin Books, 1992), p. 162.
2. Ibid.
3. Ibid., pp. 162–63.
4. Benjamin R. Foster and Karen Polinger Foster, *Civilizations of Ancient Iraq* (Princeton, New Jersey: Princeton University Press, 2009), p. 76.
5. Ibid., p. 77.
6. Ibid., p. 193.
7. C. B. Falls, *The First 3000 Years: Ancient Civilization of the Tigris, Euphrates, and Nile River Valleys, and the Mediterranean Sea* (New York: Viking Press, 1960), p. 48.

8. Ibid.

Chapter 4   Iraq and Its People
1. Wilfred Thesiger, *The Marsh Arabs* (New York: Penguin Books, 2007), p. 20.
2. Ibid., p. 7.

Chapter 5   The Waters of Babylon
1. Pearce, Fred. "Fertile Crescent 'will disappear this century.'" http://www.newscientist.com/article/dn17517-fertile-crescent-will-disappear-this-century.html
2. The Tigris & Euphrates Basin http://www.providence.edu/polisci/students/mideast_water/tigres_1.htm, p. 1
3. Ibid.
4. Water: Iraq's Other Problem http://www.circleofblue.org/waternews/2009/world/hold-water-iraqs-other-problem/, p. 1.
5. Laura Foreman, *Alexander the Conqueror: The Epic Story of the Warrior King* (Cambridge, Massachusetts: Da Capo Press, 2004), p. 145.
6. Ibid., p. 184.
7. Will Durant, *The Life of Greece.* Volume 2. The Story of Civilization (New York: Simon and Schuster, 1939), p. 548.

PHOTO CREDITS: All photos—cc-by-sa-2.0. Every effort has been made to locate all copyright holders of material used in this book. If any errors or omissions have occurred, corrections will be made in future editions of the book.

Arrian. *The Campaigns of Alexander*. Revised Edition. Translated by Aubrey de Sélincourt. New York: Penguin Books, 1971.

Code of Hammurabi
http://www.fordham.edu/halsall/ancient/hamcode.html

Cowper, Marcus. *History Book: An Interactive Journey*. Washington, D.C.: National Geographic, 2010.

Daniels, Patricia S., and Stephen G. Hyslop. *Almanac of World History*. Washington, D.C.: National Geographic, 2003.

Darwin, John. *After Tamerlane: The Global History of Empire Since 1405*. New York: Bloomsbury Press, 2008.

Durant, Will. *The Life of Greece*. Vol 2. The Story of Civilization. New York: Simon and Schuster, 1939.

Etherington, Mark. *Revolt on the Tigris: The Al-Sadr Uprising and the Governing of Iraq*. Ithaca, New York: Cornell University Press, 2005.

Falls, C. B. *The First 3000 Years: Ancient Civilization of the Tigris, Euphrates, and Nile River Valleys, and the Mediterranean Sea*. New York: Viking Press, 1960.

Foreman, Laura. *Alexander the Conqueror: The Epic Story of the Warrior King*. Cambridge, Massachusetts: Da Capo Press, 2004.

Foster, Benjamin R., and Karen Polinger Foster. *Civilizations of Ancient Iraq*. Princeton, New Jersey: Princeton University Press, 2009.

Green, Peter. *Alexander of Macedon, 356–323 B.C.: A Historical Biography*. Berkeley, California: University of California Press, 1991.

Kagan, Neil (editor). *Concise History of the World: An Illustrate Time Line*. Washington, D.C.: National Geographic, 2006.

Leick, Gwendolyn. *Mesopotamia: The Invention of the City*. New York: Penguin Books, 2001.

Mountjoy, Shane. *The Tigris and Euphrates Rivers*. Rivers in World History Series. Philadelphia, Pennsylvania: Chelsea House Publishers, 2005.

Pearce, Fred. "Fertile Crescent 'will disappear this century.'"
http://www.newscientist.com/article/dn17517-fertile-crescent-will-disappear-this-century.html

Roux, Georges. *Ancient Iraq*. Third Edition. New York: Penguin Books, 1992.

Sela, Avraham. *The Continuum Political Encyclopedia of the Middle East*. New York: Continuum, 2002.

Thesiger, Wilfred. *The Marsh Arabs*. New York: Penguin Books, 2007.

Wetlands of Iraq: Tigris-Euphrates River System, Central Marshes, Hawizeh Marshes, Hammar Marshes, Glory Canal, Lake Hammar. Memphis, Tennessee: Books LLC, 2010.

Books

Apte, Sunita. *Mesopotamia*. A True Book Series. Danbury, Connecticut: Scholastic Library Publishing, 2010.

Miller, Gary. *The Tigris and Euphrates: Rivers of the Fertile Crescent*. Rivers Around the World Series. New York: Crabtree Publishing Company, 2010.

Rowell, Rebecca. *Iraq*. Countries of the World Series. Edina, Minnesota: Abdo Publishing, 2012.

Scholl, Elizabeth. *Ancient Mesopotamia*. How'd They Do That in? Hockessin, Delaware: Mitchell Lane, 2009.

Steele, Philip. *DK Eyewitness Books: Mesopotamia*. New York: DK Publishing, 2007.

On the Internet

Geography and Maps – Ancient Mesopotamia for Kids
    http://mesopotamia.mrdonn.org/geography.html

National Geographic Kids: Iraq
    http://kids.nationalgeographic.com/Places/Find/Iraq

Social Studies for Kids: Ancient Middle East
    www.socialstudiesforkids.com/subjects/ancientmiddleeast.htm

Tigris/Euphrates River Valley Civilization
    http://www.rivervalleycivilizations.com/tigris-euphrates.php

Water: Iraq's Other Problem
    http://www.circleofblue.org/waternews/2009/world/
    hold-water-iraqs-other-problem/

alluvial (a-LOO-vi-al)—Made of soil or sand left by rivers or floods

acropolis (a-KROP-o-lis)—The citadel or fortified place in an ancient Greek city

barrage (buh-RAHZH)—An artificial barrier, especially one damming a river

basalt (ba-SAWLT)—A kind of dark rock of volcanic origin

drought (drowt)—Continuous dry weather

epicenter (EP-i-sen-ter)—The point on Earth's surface directly above the focus of an earthquake

hydroelectricity (hi-droh-i-lek-TRIS-i-tee)—Electricity produced by water power

keep (keep)—The central tower or other strongly fortified tower in a castle

mausoleum (maw-so-LEE-um)—A magnificent tomb, named for King Mausolus in Asia Minor in the fourth century BCE

minaret (min-a-RET)—A tall slender tower on or beside a mosque, with a balcony from which a muezzin calls Muslims to prayer

phalanx (FAY-langks)—A body of heavily armed infantry in ancient Greece formed in close deep ranks and files

wadi (WA-dee)—The bed or valley of a stream in regions of southwestern Asia and northern Africa that is usually dry except during the rainy season and that often forms an oasis

watchtower (WOCH-tow-er)—A tower used for observation

Zeus (zoos)—In Greek mythology, the supreme god; the "father of Gods and men"

Index

ABOUT THE AUTHOR

Earle Rice Jr. is a former senior design engineer and technical writer in the aerospace, electronic-defense, and nuclear industries. He has devoted full time to his writing since 1993 and is the author of more than 60 published books. Earle is listed in *Who's Who in America* and is a member of the Society of Children's Book Writers and Illustrators, the League of World War I Aviation Historians, the Air Force Association, and the Disabled American Veterans.